AFLOAT IN THE CONTINUUM

Collected Poems 2019-2020

by David A. Folds

WingSpan Press

Published in the United States and the United Kingdom
by WingSpan Press, Livermore, CA

The WingSpan name, logo and colophon are
the trademarks of WingSpan Publishing.

ISBN 978-1-63683-001-8 (pbk.)
ISBN 978-1-63683-998-1 (ebk.)

First edition 2021

Printed in the United States of America

www.wingspanpress.com

Library of Congress Control Number 2021

1 2 3 4 5 6 7 8 9 10

AFLOAT IN THE CONTINUUM

THIS IS DEDICATED
TO THOSE WHO GAVE ME
ENCOURAGEMENT AND DIRECTION
TO DEVELOP AND PRESENT THESE WRITINGS:
MY WIFE VICKIE
MY BROTHER CHUCK AND HIS WIFE JANE
ALAN BAXTER AND CHESTER JOHNSON
EVIE IVY AND MARVIN CAMILLO
AND JOSHUA MEANDER

The Shortest of All Streets

lower Manhattan

skyscrapers

crushed together

is still filled

with historic sites

the names of streets

still retain echoes of

over three hundred years

Pearl, Cedar, Pine,

Beaver, Water, Wall

a few of the ancient

names of streets

but what is now

the shortest of

all the city streets?

you could walk past it

and have no idea at all

1

David A. Folds

it once was three

    north-south blocks

running from Liberty

    through Cedar and Thames

        to Pine

Broadway to the east

    Trinity Place to the west

by the early nineteen hundreds

    it had been reduced

        to single block length

two large office buildings

    the Trinity and

        the U.S. Realty

were viewed

    as more important

in 1968 the remaining block

was engulfed

and erased

by the pleasant

and well used

Liberty Plaza Park

all that remains

of its old history

is a single street sign

placed on a lamp post

on the park side

by Liberty Street

there it is

unnoticed

unappreciated

but still remains

Temple Street

1/24/19 - Jersey City, NJ, USA

3   David A. Folds

The Lake

whether imagined or real

people often have

a dream place

lodged somewhere

in their memory

floating into focus

like a mysterious cloud

somewhere

off in the distance

a place they would label

as special

whether others

do or do not

such a place for me

was Lauderdale Lakes

when my father was young

about 1920

his father bought

a cottage

in lower Wisconsin

on Green Lake

it was at one end

of three connected siblings

they were together named

Lauderdale Lakes

Their cottage was

one of only three

on the entire lake system

all around there was nothing

but green brown woods

David A. Folds

my father learned to hunt there

from an uncle with numerous

trophy heads

eventually dad stopped that

finding no love

for killing

by my time every available lot space

was owned and housed

even two lots away

from the water

from when I was

first in school

we would spend

a few weeks

each summer

up there

for me in the back seat

of our hand-me-down car

going up and down

the rolling hills

on what was then

a two hour drive

was almost like

a milder roller-coaster

enjoying that and

the occasional clever

Burma Shave Signs

the cottage was enlarged

over time

seated upon a

partially wooded hill

overlooking

the green peace

below us

David A. Folds

by my time it had

two stories

with four bedrooms

upstairs

as well as a sleeping porch

that could take

three more beds

overlooking the water was

a screened porch

as wide as the cottage

a place for calm

and quiet

but overhearing

sounds from the lake

occasional voices

a passing motorboat

the whole family

would gather

for my Granddad's

birthday

and all could be housed

and fed

everyone seated at the large

dining room table

I always was seated

to the left of my

left-handed cousin

both of us

trying to not bang elbows

David A. Folds

every day there was

morning and afternoon

swim time

we kids would be in and out

of the softly rolling waves

until meal time

or until parents said

come out now

your lips are starting

to turn blue

we could not argue with that

my brother and my two female cousins

would pass in-between swim time

with playing Monopoly, Clue,

or Canasta

a four-person card game

popular in the 1950s

much later now I have a phone app

that has that game

once all but Granddad

sitting a distance away

reading

played a family game

of charades

and Grandma stole the show

leaving us all

in stitches

she should have been on stage

David A. Folds

she was the real foundation

of the family

strongly in control

of the household

often outspoken

while her husband remained

quietly dignified

our mothers had

housekeeping duties

including cooking

while our fathers were

as free as us youngsters

of course we loved it the most

swimming and playing

in the enveloping lake water

or out in a rowboat

or better yet

a canoe

gave us a feeling

that peace was all there was

floating swimming

wrapped in the blue-green

almost amniotic liquid

touched the memory

of a former calm

within the womb

David A. Folds

we could describe

everything about it

name the three lakes

the town nearby

show the location

on the map

and the route

to get there

but among ourselves

there was no need to say

anything more than

the lake

2/18/19 - Jersey City, NJ, USA

The Body and Beyond

the body is my vehicle

all through

my life

amazing in its DNA

created complexity

cells replacing cells

continuously

sensors declaring

the good the bad

and the dangerous

synaptic messages

leap from

one brain cell

on to the next

David A. Folds

but

existing within this vehicle

there is still more

than the doctors

and scientists

can account for

the Chinese

speak of Chi

a mysterious

flow of energy

within the body

and the world

around it

acupuncture

uses that force

activating energy points

increasing the inner Chi

as do ancient practices

like Tai Chi Ch'uan

in India

    they talk of Chakras

their version of

    energy centers

when they try to

    awaken the coiled

        sleeping snake

          of Kundalini

the energy waiting to

    rise up

    shooting through

        each higher Chakra

    to the top

    of the head

bursting into

    the Crown Chakra

    creating a bliss

        beyond normal

        imaginings

David A. Folds

in the span of

our lives

we function within

our body's experience

and the outside world

that contacts our senses

while our brains

try to choose what

to ignore

what to give focus

but beyond that

seek to find

the hidden

the mysterious

searching for

a higher meaning

an answer

at the heart

of our existence

3/13/19 - Jersey City, NJ, USA

Afloat in the Continuum

18

Images Out of Focus

the frost of my memory

beckons from beyond

my floating thoughts

what happened long before

echoes softly

in and out of focus

when the present

dulls and slows

almost to a halt

I live with

moments of

magic

like scenes

from a haunting film

David A. Folds

disconnected

　　but flowing

　　　　in and out of

　　　　　　my crowded mind's eye

the times of our being

　　are instant

　　　　collages

　　of now and then and maybe

while we look towards

　　a promise of a future

　　　　still with mystery

3/25/19 - Jersey City, NJ, USA

The Touch of a Dog

just outside

City Hall Park

my wife and I

came upon them

a lady walking

an obviously

elderly retriever

the old one walking

with probably

arthritic pain

and Vickie spoke to the lady

to ask the age of her dog

as she was fifteen

I had to reply

that she was very old

for a larger breed

David A. Folds

this retriever

a female

looked at me

and without prodding

presented my left hand

with a loving touch

of her tongue

the sweetness of the gesture

still resonates

with me now

4/10/19 - Jersey City, NJ, USA

After St. Mathew Passion Poem

how can I understand

how can I bare

   my small burden

how can I understand

   how huge

      the burden is

         for me

I am not innocent

  I am not pure

how can I understand

   how Christ gave himself

      to his destruction

      to despair

         to torturous death

  from a purity

     of all eternity all time

David A. Folds

amazingly this was done

for me and for all mankind

it was beyond the belief

the comprehension

of all his disciples

that his earthly being

would soon be erased

in earthly shame

and eternal glory

how can I understand

can you?

the son of man

a target of envy

but also of fear

an innocent in the den

of scribes and priests

could not be given

the freedom to preach

to heal

to show them

their weaknesses

and failures

foolishly they had thought

his death

could wash away

the embarrassment

the intrusion to their

established power

but they understood

even less than I

4/25/19 - Jersey City, NJ, USA

David A. Folds

Mist

the soft murmur

    of the morning mist

awaits the rise

    of human activity

adds an invisible veil

    a filter to the atmosphere

gives a slightly damp look

    to barks of trees and leaves

spreads its moist dew

    across the thankful grass

only to be baked away

    eventually

cooked by the insistent

    inevitable

    rays of light

5/18/19 - Jersey City, NJ, USA

Moment of a Poem

a whirlwind of

meandering thoughts

surrounds and invades

my inner being

particles of images

float in

and laugh

phrases dance in

forte or sotto voce

until the ideas find some

strength

some point of

recognition

David A. Folds

words step forward

demanding their time

their moment to

spring the trap

to release a flow

even perhaps

a spurt of

thoughts painted

in the structure

in a creation

of our Americanized

English

4/23/19 - Jersey City, NJ, USA

My Song to You

the morning wakes

    my song to you

a chorus of

    vibrant slivers of light

        invading the quiet

          darkness

urging, massaging, stirring

    my consciousness

        away from floating dreams

but now a door is opened

    and my mind floats

      through it

while I feel you also stirring

    next to me

David A. Folds

and I know

    our life is a song

       of many verses

      many notes and some dissonance

but within it all

    floating free

will be

    my song to you

6/4/19 - Jersey City, NJ, USA

Moments in Time

the shadow of forgotten plans

echoes faintly

across my mind

dipping heals and toes

below the murky

liquid of unknown

waters passing by

moments arriving

unannounced

as they do

not waiting for response

but gone, forgotten too

and I wonder what

keeps me together

David A. Folds

in this multiplexed

chaotic demanding world

time washes over

erasing minutes

gone

forgotten, flowing out of focus

faded behind some other moment

arriving quickly

and forever gone

6/23/19 - Jersey City, NJ, USA

Krems

in Austria

I grew amazed

on a stroll

in the beautiful

main streets of Krems

you could never

have imagined

so many interesting

three story buildings

each with its own

ground floor shop

or restaurant

or café

David A. Folds

each of these

with its own particular

design and colors

and signs

how could it be that

every owner had acquired

such an excellent sense

of visual taste?

anyone of them

if they were less

would have stood out

embarrassed

like an ugly wound

but I saw no such wounds

the feeling was both peaceful

and vibrant

alive and in balance

8/5/19 - Krems, Austria

Praha

here in America

    we know it as Prague

their "ha" approximates

    a "gue" to us

for those in the new world

    never having experienced it

it is an exotic city

    lost in the fog

        of our version

        of history

which loves Western

    and largely ignores

        Eastern Europe

Paris and Rome

    and Venice

    are deservedly darlings

but Prague is a jewel

    whose sights can

    overwhelm eyes and minds

David A. Folds

old areas away from the sleek

modern sectors

are full of buildings

of four stories

each with its own

color and character

many standing hundreds of years

the churches with

distinctive Eastern European

dark spires

vaulting above

the tops of other buildings

almost shouting

projecting

pointing up to Heaven

and views from the Charles Bridge

that overwhelm

on the bridge itself

and even more

looking out

from the bridge railings

to either side

a complex beauty

at whatever angle

of the river below

and the buildings on shore

your camera in time

must span

three hundred

and sixty degrees

all along this bridge

it is a unique

visual feast

David A. Folds

from the twenty-fourth floor

of my modern hotel

the richness of the sights

in all directions

speak to the need

to come and experience

come and learn that

your life had been

lacking this awareness

this vibrancy

8/11/19 - on the flight from Prague, Czech Republic

Sunset

from blue white

to orange yellow red

the skies of early evening

broiled by the unforgiving

oven of afternoon

summer heat

sing a song of

nature's paintings

gifts of visions

glory to those observing

magic moments

David A. Folds

if one can only stop

halting the day's

aggression

briefly absorbing

magic in a small

time of wonder

8/22/19 Jersey City, NJ, USA

The Hudson

the song of the boats

flowing across the water

this one north

two others south

add accents to

the wide always

moving Hudson

from a nearby window

this scene presents

a calm that

peaceful waters bring

the passion within

the river

never reaches the

space between

the slats of my blinds

David A. Folds

only the soft

    motion of

        distant water

      echoes its soothing

      rhythm

time passing

     river moving on

8/23/19 Jersey City, NJ, USA

It's For You

years ago

    there was man

        a black man in his thirties

    who would walk about

      here and there

        throughout

        lower Manhattan

perhaps he was not entirely

    there mentally

but he would carry

    in one hand

        the receiver for

        a landline phone

dangling from it was

    its severed short cord

      connecting to nothing

David A. Folds

he would talk to it

continuously

until he would choose

an unsuspecting partner

walk towards the person

to hand them the phone

saying

it's for you

at some point

the advent

of the cell phone

killed his gig

9/5/19 Jersey City, NJ, USA

Natural Awareness

I do not know the names

of the flora and fauna

in my experiences

unlike Carlos Williams who

seemed intimately aware

of trees and bushes

and birds

he would pass them

noting their current state

the colors of the moment

shapings and

the inevitable futures

as seasons would mold and

feed and then destroy

here the trees continue

slowly larger

flowers are planted

in landscaping

David A. Folds

and birds gather

in one heavily

covered tree

in the evening

chirping in a mighty

chorus

while geese and ducks

come to land

for favorite foods

no longer only scouring

the river for their meals

yes I move among

the gifts of nature

but with my focus

mostly toward

the next experience

of this life's menu

9/12/19 Jersey City, NJ, USA

Invisible Film

to beat the drums

    of sorry songs

to trample in the slush

    of melting snow

in motion -- moving forward

    without reason

      without rhyme

everything revolves around us

    ignored near or far

the first steps outside

    bright burst of sunlight

    breath of unconditioned air

      throw open a wider world

David A. Folds

we stride breaking past

each open moment

experiences rejected

only focused on a path

a journey a target

perhaps a job

an errand or a date

flowing through the

soft cells in our minds

is an unending film

of life around us

we hardly ever recognize

10/16/19 Jersey City, NJ, USA

Listening

the tripped tiptoes

of table talk

wash over fading pains

the panacea of the populous

some smooth spoken

others blared out boldly

force momentary focus

on prosaic thoughts

just spoken out loud

invading the quiet

words as sound

connecting with others

forming something perhaps

such that perhaps

we should listen

10/4/19 Plane from Tacloban, Leyte, Philippines to Cebu City, Cebu, Philippines

David A. Folds

Sunday Train

taking the PATH

    to Herald Square

on a Sunday morning

    dressed for Church

I encounter unusual numbers

    on the platform

        on the side for the city

many must be tourists

    lodged in Jersey

here to see some of the

    annual marathon run

my arthritic knees

    can not welcome

    even the idea

        of running on any

        hard mineral surface

and they forget

    that the poor man

        who ran the original

           in Greece

    ran it under

        ultimate orders

when the train comes

    I know where to stand

        where the door opens

even so I am

    like a sardine

        crammed into a shiny can

packed with a happy

    crowd hoping

        to view something special

David A. Folds

while I will subway

downtown

still early for Service

not focused on athletics

and physical stress

wishing for guidance

and some peace

11/5/2019   Jersey City, NJ, USA

Morning Heat

the warmth of sunlit morn

masks the cold

of selfish yearning

a brief moment

of a chorus

of nature singing

heat assaults

embraces our being

shiny surroundings

quick absorption

in a peripheral scan

quickly passed over

discarded

David A. Folds

replaced by the need for now

the reason we

ventured out

focus on the small immediate

direction's demand

11/13/2019   Jersey City, NJ, USA

Christmas in November

it is a winter's warming story

wrapped in tinfoil

like some heated chestnuts

shifts of the wind

reshuffle and re-deal

the scattered snow

trees stripped naked

flail empty twigs and branches

swaying to a meandering breeze

David A. Folds

but we have intervened

breaking the stark season's

cold facade

with bright lights of

the distant holiday

reds and blues

greens and yellows and white

beaming in brightness

unavoidable

indelibly changing

the late autumn

spirit

11/13/2019 Jersey City, NJ, USA

Others

it is less than pity

    and more than more

the sweet savage surge

    of restless brotherhood

        caught in a moment

capital I becoming briefly small

we swim mostly in our

    experience of instances

internally gathered

    then pushed aside

in the center of our

    microcosmic existence

ignoring the overwhelming

    vastness of layer

        upon layer

           of larger worlds

David A. Folds

reach out with open hand

to embrace the other

the anonymous trees and shrubs

the solar rise and fall

the other

the person not yet

known to you

11/16/2019   Jersey City, NJ, USA

Beyond Never

when will never come again

echoes fade

and memories soften

as sweetness sours

relentless time devours

all our favorite focus

moments quickly turn

to nothing

no growth emerges

out of never

nothing beckons

near or far

David A. Folds

but we walk onward

moment to moment

striding forward

for a sense of hope

a hope for something

out of nothing

beyond our never

past our nothing

hoping to flow into

a newness dawning

burning bright

11/25/2019   Jersey City, NJ, USA

Sight in the Light

the love of light

    reflects the absence

      of darkness

images on display

    everywhere

      a detailed collage

where even the shaded sights

    in the shadows

      give off softened forms

without the glow

    of the impact

      of direct radiance

peripheral sight

    gathers colorings

    and shapes

David A. Folds

not clearly defined

but absorbed

like an impersonal

smorgasbord

slightly tasted

but thrown aside

while we want only

the direct focus

the aim of our

bi-vision eyes

12/11/2019   Jersey City, NJ, USA

Travel Inside

walk through

the quiet places

of your mind

as water shifts with tides

and winds

while wind chimes awaken

some ancient memories

not lost, but hidden

beneath layers of

common repetitions

find the calm

of total focus

David A. Folds

all internal

    radiating outward

inside is the root

    that leads to peace

to erase the chaos

    of external influence

peace if only

    for one brief time

for a brief time

    or perhaps for more

12/27/2019 Jersey City, NJ, USA

Sunlight and Wind

all the work of the wind

    passes without a sigh

ruffled hair

    fluttering scarves

        waving flags

            shivering branches

and unrepentant time

    moves on

        just as quickly

while bleaching rays of the sun

    burst past every twist

        of the wind

heating the pavement

    and the skin

David A. Folds

now time accumulates

the repetitions of

each moment of heat

each impact of breeze

gaining a collection

of experience

as each step

strides towards

seconds yet to come

1/20/2020 Jersey City, NJ, USA

The Last Phase

in the old people's home

in his last stages

my father was housed

in a hospital like room

with all his earthly possessions

a closet full of clothes

a bureau with some more

and also various things

in the lower drawers

on a wall two rows of books

and a few remaining

paintings

on the other

so that this comprised

a diminished view

of his contracted

shrinking experience

David A. Folds

he still could speak expertly

about the art

look to the art related

books and magazines

and remember many

rich experiences

gathered during

over 95 years

he treasured our visits

loved sharing moments

with a son

marveled at a daughter-in-law

who climbed on to a chair

to neatly rearrange

all the books

and he still saw life as a gift

a treasure continuing

until done

1/20/2020   Jersey City, NJ, USA

Paths of Options

under the umbrella of chance

we took a different path

not knowing the why

or the wherefore

and by this chance

we saw something different

or something familiar

like a long-lost friend

or we met someone from our past

with echoes of old experiences

almost forgotten

pulling away from our forward rush

with the usual blinders

that exclude the vastness

of the possible

David A. Folds

freedom practiced

for those who have the chance

to be free

should be an obligation

to oneself

to breathe the open radiance

both outside and

deep within

2/9/2020   Jersey City, NJ, USA

Mother and the Dog

when I was fifteen

we took in a dog

for the first time

in my life

my father learned that

a woman clerking

in a supermarket

had a female two year old

mixed breed

but could not keep her

my mother named her Sukero

from Italian for sweet

and we quickly shortened that

to Sukie

Sukie had been spaded

after one litter of pups

David A. Folds

having gone through birth

and being female

she was very caring

especially so because

she was grateful to be out of

that dog shelter

whenever in our car

sensing we were headed

even in the direction of that shelter

she would whine

pityingly

my mother being a homemaker

spent much more time

with this loving canine

as she went to various parts

of our house

Sukie would follow along

but a favorite spot was

on the flat top

of a closed sewing machine

there lying on a towel

she could look out the window

and if the window was open

could smell much more than us

in the afternoon

she would know when

I was coming from school

when still blocks away

and if we were out of the house

for a number of hours

when we returned

she would joyfully

greet us

but she would have

taken some tissue

from a wastebasket

ripping it up

and leaving it

by the door

as a protest

David A. Folds

my parents moved to New York

in the Spring of 1960

now being apartment dwellers

it was not a good place

for the dog

before moving

they found a local family

that would lovingly

keep her

two years later

I was home when

my mother opened

a letter from them

as Sukie had developed a cancer

she had been

put to sleep

my mother cried deep tears

that day

2/11/2020   Jersey City, NJ, USA

Cosmic Questions

lasting into the

    laughing shake

        of eternal moments

we pause with

    one foot raised

        unsure of where

            to land

we feel half inside

    but half away

        from the balance

            of our being

pulled up ... pulled down

    we drain our

        vital energy

will the wind answer

    the question of direction

can the brilliant light of Sol

    spark an inner flame

David A. Folds

yes, but energy

without direction

collapses into chaos

marriage of the two

in a moment of completeness

seems all too foreign and

just unreachable

why this is so?

we are

our only enemies

building all the barriers

keeping out the peace

2/14/2020   Jersey City, NJ, USA

Modern Times

while the chimes of change

    ring far off key

we step into a new day

    much like a day before

as beauty still exists

    outside our bunkered buildings

      and metropolitan spaces

utility for humans

    creates artifices

      of steel and stone

asphalt and cement replacing

    soil and grass

      become our walkways

David A. Folds

the pulse of nature

still felt by us

comes from the rays

of the sun

and the atmosphere

that is beginning

to be altered

by us

the flow of life

becomes too complex

a thing for simple nature

it seems that we

just can't

leave it alone

2/26/2020   Jersey City, NJ, USA

The Smallest of Lives

the moon throbs

    soft memories of love

as drifting cloud configurations

    filter the images of thought

shifting winds buffet

    first one side of my head

        and then the other

pointing to this

    and then to that

        direction of

            a moment in life

we are complacent

    in our appreciation

        of the chances of choices

we move onward to

    … something

David A. Folds

bodies toting our minds

while our souls

continue

an unseen connection

our stride seems to

draw our energy

onward to new

awakenings

but in perspective

it's as though

our stride stands still

an iota in the largesse

of time and space

3/7/2020   Jersey City, NJ, USA

Mid-Century Evanston

I grew up in Evanston

in the 1940's and 50's

the town perched right above

the top of Chicago

its east end along the upper

west coast of the

mighty Lake Michigan

we lived in the somewhat

idealistic, naive,

post-war, television

emerging,

Christian based

society

still learning

what we were

what we needed to become

David A. Folds

of all the North Shore suburbs

Evanston was the only one

where Blacks could find housing

they could work throughout

the North Shore

but they could only live

in Evanston or Chicago itself

mind you, at that time

even Evanston and Chicago

still had limitations

both had their Black sections

and their larger White areas

but all teenagers went to one

large township high school

integrated classes

in an only partly

integrated society

I heard from a friend

as a senior in '59

that two Black male seniors

had dated two white girls

I was shocked to hear

that some ass-holes had

burned a cross before

the home of one

of the girls

many years later I learned that

family had

quickly moved away

David A. Folds

the YMCA I went to

was then White only

in the Black section

there was a Black "Y"

at one meeting of my "Y" club

we discussed this issue

opinions varied among us boys

some still believed that

separate could be equal

others like me

saw it as unequal, unfair

we were still trying to climb

sometimes I felt thankful to be

growing up in the North

not where slavery

had been rampant

as a child I never even

reached as far south as

Central Illinois

all this was earlier

than the time

when the struggle

for universal equality

grew strength

in the 1960's

David A. Folds

I wanted the world

to have true value

to all people

but had yet to discover

how to achieve more

than simple equality

for all those in my daily

journeys, trials, and tests

today I am still trying to learn

3/31/2020   Jersey City, NJ, USA

Spaces

in the distant somewhere

    that I have never been

jagged cliffs and peaks

    ascend almost out of sight

mossy green too high for trees

    reach up until

the snow and ice

    freeze out all

        but the rock itself

too high for breath

    too cold for life

but a very few seek

    to climb

        to reach the top

as though such action

    actually could conquer it

David A. Folds

we look to dominate

    all things in the physical

even outer space

    compared to which

        we are

            just infinitesimal

seek instead the

    undefinable

    the space within

4/4/2020   Jersey City, NJ, USA

Unaware

a day that you

     will never remember

         just passed

like a phantom mist

     leaving only echoes

         that are just ignored

asked what it was

     what really occurred

you scratch the top

     of your scalp

or finger your

     uncommitted chin

wondering now what it was

     where it really went

David A. Folds

dawn brings on a new

anonymous Sun

distributing zillions

of seeking searching

rays of energy

unintentionally

they try to stir us

to awaken a new

depth of awareness

4/4/2020   Jersey City, NJ, USA

Eye of the Mind

looking from the window

of my mind

passing images of thought

stream by

like views from a

fast moving train

closing my eyes

to try to slow

the progression

engulfed in yellow orange

darkness

eyelids pressed

against the lenses

a deep full breath

energizes

the peace

time is becoming quiet

but still is moving on

4/5/2020 Jersey City, NJ, USA

David A. Folds

Time Uncaring

the bloom of lost blossoms

has faded away

the long-suppressed sighs

of past frustrations

have returned

while the flow of time

does not trip or stumble

but we do as we slip into

distracted moments

but time surges forward

uncaring if we

are passed by

each day brings new

chances and challenges

problems and choices

what results will be reached

only time will tell

4/12/2020   Jersey City, NJ, USA

Our Dance of Life

to sing the soft sounds

of sorrow

while fate laughs away

at our futilely

we are like single cells

in the body

of existence

as in our own bodies

cells develop, flower,

wither and die

and are replaced

David A. Folds

that does not show

our creator's

lack of caring

we have our chance

to dance

our moments of minutes

of flesh

our time to

gather self

to flow in the

universal river

of time

an instance

brought into union

merging with the

pulse of eternity

breathing the timelessness

of the rhythm

of the word

5/6/2020 Jersey City, NJ, USA

Afloat in the Continuum

Inner Strength

winds wind through

thoughts of change

memories float fuzzy visions

of past participles

and people pass through

moments of the

soft fogs

of their lives

waiting, but not waiting,

for something of strength

some way to spread past

their daily grind

what vision, what path

is calling?

David A. Folds

the expanse of our

small bit of universe

is a mote within

a mote

of space

our world's expanse

within a universe

as one of how many

worlds still

unseen, unknown?

one tries to stretch

expand experience

embracing more

and still more spheres

of the cosmos

until, perhaps,

looking deep within

to find a universe

of unity

complete inside

5/12/2020   Jersey City, NJ, USA

Love and Union

love locked in chaos

    flies high in intensity

fast flying dramas

    too short to absorb

balanced on edge

    shaking knees buckle

away from the normal

    safe moments of life

when the passion is cut

    like a trapdoor falling

all balance implodes

    and a passion of loss

turns the heart swift to ice

    turns a mind soft to mush

with focus unstable

    unable to breathe

what could have happened?

    how will life proceed?

David A. Folds

I've been there before

but not for a long time

now I'm still blessed

with our constant relation

feeling grounded

with strength

while we're wrapped

in the passion

of our peace

5/15/2020   Jersey City, NJ, USA

Afloat in the Continuum

Now and Future

winding words through

jungles of thought

the meaning stumbles

and focus blurs

we dance until the music stops

we sing to raise

the dead momentum

the dawn of days

beacon beaming

searches all

the quiet moments

stirs the sleeping

peaceful plants

heats the dampness

from the dew

blanketing over everything

a Canadian goose fluffs its feathers

awakening the muscles of its neck

David A. Folds

web feet waddle

into water

floating buoyant

peaceful glide

dog walkers following

the leader

leashes stretched

well before them

blinking eyelids that are

newly awakened

as early morning glare

thins the visual gap

the day is early but growing fast

the future is now but still yet to come

what will we climb

what will we deliver

the manifestations of our reality await

wait and truly tremble

6/3/2020   Jersey City, NJ, USA

Aging

I am in the summer

of my winter

each day's a small hill

to climb

each night's a quiet cove

to beach

age is a quagmire

of contradictions

you are as young as you think

and as old as you feel

most mornings awake

just like Saturday

only Sunday differs

because of church

I am no longer a profession

I am no longer a job

David A. Folds

my identity now tied to

what I did before

and what I never did

no longer to seek

the dynamic

but search for some

peace and beauty

the clock still clicks just the same

as when I was a child

but my awareness

of it is greater

and I remain in

the dance of life

low blood pressure at 79

6/11/2020   Jersey City, NJ, USA

Life's Montague

we trip through

    the land of knowledge

and swim in a sea

    of ignorance

each step unbalancing

    as a raised foot

reaches the next forward

    target to nowhere

passing between quick clips

    of fading films

dreams floating away

    like clouds

we look for the upturned

    praise of success

no matter how unimportant

    the deed

David A. Folds

the routine of daily living

grounds us

but it floats

on stagnant waters

we eat to live

we live to think

to remember

to forget

to laugh

to cry

how can we be the artists

to sculpt a union

of meaning to our

fading moments?

6/23/2020   Jersey City, NJ, USA

Lost in 1964

after traversing a blazing

purple afternoon

time to step into the mystery

of the unknown

drop down below the Village

of change

into somewhere later known

as north of Tribeca

in a casual lounging

jazz joint

with no charge at the

Half Note door

come in find a table

or just sit at the bar

David A. Folds

the narrow platform

is right behind

where Sonny or Mike is bartending

you can sip a drink or two for hours

with great music

staring back at you

players like Coltrane and Wes Montgomery

singers like Anita O'Day and Jimmy Rushing

but almost a house band was Al and Zoot

two tenor saxes and

a good rhythm section

Sonny or Mike would feed them whiskey

in shot glasses

in between numbers

there they would stand

holding the glasses

until finally deciding to drink

and then just drop it

every time Sonny or Mike had to catch

else there was broken glass

on the floor

music flowing and swinging

free from commercialism

of the music business

David A. Folds

in the main dining table space

a small aging waiter reigned

he could be at the kitchen door

when at the other end

of the room

a guy would be readying a match

to light his girl's smoke

but before he could do it

this waiter would get there first

lighter lit and ready

at that time there was none of that

cover charge crap

and wait on line for one set crap

the music filled the dusky space

and you were there

seated floating free

6/27/2020   Jersey City, NJ, USA

Afloat in the Continuum

Awaiting

the icicles on the branches

hang heavy

a hope for freezing rain

but the warmer days

loosen their frozen grip

gradually dripping

down to half chilled dirt

now branches await their freedom

their chance to

bring forth buds

to burst out new life

the heat above spreads

insistent warmth

of a penetrating sun

demanding a new time

a new awakening

David A. Folds

listen

the birds begin to sing

of Spring

they would laugh

if they could

they flit about

in a search

of scarce food

the flowering of new growth

will help feed them soon

small life will crawl and creep

or fly into their happy craws

to feed demanding chicks

too young to sing of the

fast flight of life

the ground softens

the branches bloom

nature smiles again

7/10/2020   Jersey City, NJ, USA

Brief Baptism

a clear bright morn

      sparked spirits to song

the flow of existence

      seemingly in balance

heat leaped off windows

      metallically insistent

reflected rays of second

      hand light

a bouquet of fresh breath

      stirred muscles and sinew

what more could there be

      what more could we want

but every gift precedes a penalty

every penalty is truly a gift

as midday tripped past

      a white to gray then black

      ceiling of clouds

      slid slowly east

David A. Folds

dispersing our friendly

range of comfort

atmosphere now clogged

deep in humidity

awaiting a promised

full onslaught

until quickly

drops descended

a communal bath

begun

baptism chose

a new beginning

all wet washed

to clean

as the rain rejoiced

midst a chorus

of thunder

7/11/2020   Jersey City, NJ, USA

Limitations

let us stroll

let us ponder

the flowing green

of wild grass

rolling hills in small

undulations

to the side thick forest

of pine and oak

a healthy hike

over and through

the soft welcome of

unmowed wildness

rising slowly

to not a peak

but an abrupt stoppage

of earth at cliffside edge

a drop off down

to rocky sand

David A. Folds

breakers storming

      the stony barrier

at their chosen

      rhythmic intervals

spaced sequences

      of advancing waves

mimic the rise and

      fall behind us

of hills that seem

      to move but

never reaching

      to meet the waves

never searching

      the deep mystery

of blue green

      liquid vastness

never traveling

      far outward

to dance in the horizon

to sing in the song of the rising sun

7/27/2020 Jersey City, NJ, USA

Reverberations

and the bells resound

flying into every space

and nook and crevice

bathing all with a wash

of awakening

tonal trembling

vibrations for everyone

for everything

a moment shared by all

with no denial

no refusal

inescapable

even felt on the skin

of those who

can not hear

creating moments

of shared experience

David A. Folds

it is the church bells

tolling the new hour

they would wish to

gather us

to pull everyone into

the entryway

to worship

but we are locked

in earlier laid plans

away to a next encounter

off to necessary business

afoot on

a new adventure

lost in a progression

of mundane moments

but the bells bathe our being

in bright hues of sound

briefly a few seconds

uplifted in tone

8/7/2020   Jersey City, NJ, USA

Happiness

there is a mystery

    to the dawn of happiness

the light of the lifting of sorrow

    peeks through

shining vibrations

    at the speed of light

flowing through every

    corpuscle

a smile becomes

    inevitable

a laugh echoes through

    each and every brain cell

for a time the misery

    of imbalance and doubt

        will be wiped clean

and the seconds flow

    to minutes

        without stumbling

David A. Folds

in the belief of the

presence of peace

and balance

until something

tips over the scale

and we are left looking

for a way

to land our ship away

from disturbing waters

a safe haven

to breath slowly deep

and stroll cleanly

to a calm

8/12/2020   Jersey City, NJ, USA

Vickie

there is a direct line

from 1979

at the UN Badminton Club

to our lives

together today

one summer evening

I saw her for

the first time

she was on court

and wore

a t-shirt that said

It's Me

somehow then

I knew that it was

David A. Folds

this small very pretty

Philippine lady

who was just being ---

not full of herself

I got to know

gradually

when she knew

I worked in a

photographic lab

she asked for

some help

she had a new Nikon

she could reasonably

reach forward

she was a little shy

certainly not aggressive

after play I would see her

to her uptown bus

days later I asked

for a date

by then her feet were covered

bunion operations on both

we walked eight blocks to

a beautiful Italian movie

"The Tree of Wooden Clogs"

the first steps were taken

towards a lifelong path

we were in it

for the long haul

in it for all tomorrows

8/13/2020 Jersey City, NJ, USA

David A. Folds

The Duke

he grew up middle class

in still racist DC

planned to be an artist

with a brush

but the haunting rhythmic pulse

of early jazz piano

waylaid those plans

so he had to learn

from the best

Lucky Roberts, Eubie Blake

a little later James P. Johnson

Fats Waller, Willie the Lion Smith

by 1927 now a band leader

featured at the Cotton Club

playing what was advertised as

jungle music

band, dancers and singers

all for a white-only crowd

building repertoire continually

learning to write and play

with a singular genius

his copywritten tunes so popular

their income

sustained his band

even during the lean

post-war 1940s

when good bands disbanded

or shrunk in size

he could awaken

in the middle of his sleep

jot down music thoughts

and hear his band play

new ideas next day

David A. Folds

creativity kept rolling

and climbing to new heights

until the wear and tear

of itinerant music life

left him with a body

no longer able to strive

only able to pray

and look fondly

towards the beyond

he passed in 1974

I think he knew

we loved him madly

8/25/2020 Jersey City, NJ, USA

Anthem

I can sing softly

    of the sinking psalms

        of lost tomorrows

I can walk through

    the decrepit alleyways

        view rats in search of food

but let us float briefly

    above it for

        a moment of reflection

sunlight breathing energy

    into lethargic dance

a kind wind

    presents an offering

        air revitalizing awareness

David A. Folds

we walk in unassuming space

to float between

clouds of doubt and

rivers of sorrow

now is the only moment

then is just abstraction

step towards your center

listen to the ballads of beauty

above the floating thoughts

9/3/2020 Jersey City, NJ, USA

Kundalini 1971

the guru said do this

in the meditation

focus first on the lower

base of the spine

with focus rising within the spine

up to below the navel

now focus rising

to the solar plexus

next flow up to the heart

and then to the throat

rising up to the mysterious

third eye

in the temple

between your temples

finally culminating

in a spread through

the upper crown

David A. Folds

I did not think about it

I just did it

unexplained

unbelievable

energy

flowing up this channel

from base to crown

shortly I

that is my consciousness

was up to the

two story ceiling

looking down at

myself and others

in meditative pose

until some time passing

returned me to my

body consciousness

in some ways

I was forever changed

impossible now

to disbelieve

only later did I learn

that the do this

instructions

were for the generally

unattainable

elusive

yoga of Kundalini

guided by a guru's

spiritual energy

a gift of understanding

to never go away

9/7/2020   Jersey City, NJ, USA

David A. Folds

In the Grip of a Pandemic

the ethereal presence of

moving cloud formations

look down and laugh

at our static

fragile mortality

they can be anywhere

be anything

evolving quickly

here in a moment

and then gone forgotten

we live in a usual

feeling of power

the life blood flow

rebuilding

renewing strength

our physical and

mental creations

seeming to magnify

exponentially

our control over

this often

unforgiving universe

even when the chemistry

of existence

heaves a deadly missile

into the heart

of human breath

we look we hope for

an eventual solution

as people act responsibly

while others

sneer at that

and more seem semi

ignorant of the mortal danger

David A. Folds

the negative reactions

win at least for now

as it takes only a few

to spread the poison

control is sporadic

inconsistent

from place to place

led by a fool

in Washington

no standard

for behavior

is national

our eyes look up in frustration

our arms shaking

in helpless anger

while the clouds

look down and laugh

9/29/2020   Jersey City, NJ, USA

Memories

the moonlight

    of forgotten times

washes over moments

    of stalled momentum

standing swaying

    still uncommitted

thoughts fly forth

    images blurred

        and fleeting

experiences lost

    discarded

erased by

    the motion

        of the movement

    of time

David A. Folds

we feel a connection

are apart

of these yesterdays

but we can not taste

or touch them

our lives are forever

imprisoned

in the tyranny

of the present

no wish can

wash away

the meaning of now

10/8/2020   Jersey City, NJ, USA

Moments of Magic

in the 1980s

we flew out

to visit

to reconnect

with relatives

long not seen

but not forgotten

in the Midwest

of my childhood

at the summer home

of family

seated in lower

Wisconsin

a chance to turn

back time

to July 4th

occurred

David A. Folds

up there that day

had rained out

all chance to

celebrate

the replacement

date was now

at hand

Vickie and I

aunt and uncle

cousin and husband

and baby of one

and not to forget

my aunt's

mother of 100

all loaded at twilight

into two boats

to traverse the waters

from our lake

through one and then

a second

connected lake

to gather on water

beneath the stars

for a magical

night of fireworks

no other celebration

of independence

could ever match

the beauty

of this explosion

of joy and wonder

10/8/2020 Jersey City, NJ, USA

David A. Folds

Birthing Growth

beginning midst the twisted

    strands of roots of trees

green bursts up

    from hard cold earth

        to seek the sun

stalk stems

    arise to climb

        high enough

for side limbs to emerge

    for leaves and

        even blossoms

            eventually to appear

we remember

    few birth or early moments

the times merge

    the development

and blur or erase

    images of memory

we become a

      a conglomerate

of youth and age

      a mixed salad

            of our old and

                  new experiences

who is this one

      seated deep

            inside me

this one I seem

      to know but

            am never sure

the limbs have grown

      and weathered

            storms

David A. Folds

leaves of perception

still gather the

light from life

occasional blossoms

will appear

to pollinate

a complex

world of

creativity

and the stems and limbs

and flowers

will still continue on

until a cold harshness

forces a retreat

10/17/2020   Jersey City, NJ, USA

Morning Work

first the blueberries

    choose and clean

        enough for two

divide them equally

    placed in two bowls

choose the strawberries

    enough for two

clean and dice

    in half dime size

divided equally

    in just the same way

clean the avocado

    cut down to the pit

        slicing in half

half for now

    half for tomorrow

David A. Folds

cuts by length

    and then by width

dividing equally

    a fourth

        to each bowl

clean the banana

    peal down to half

half for now

    half for tomorrow

cut down halfway

    twice

        creating four parts

slice half of the half

    to one bowl

        and half to the other

clean the yellow mango

cut one side

top to bottom

close to the pit

dice the cut side

scoop out half

to one bowl

half to the other

now all that's left to add

will be some milk

and perhaps some sugar

to complete a breakfast

bounteous beginning

10/23/2020   Jersey City, NJ, USA

David A. Folds

Signs

I am the archer

half man half horse

with sharp

drawn bow

some will have

an aim to

the flat horizon

others like me

have our angle

elevated

shooting towards

the infinity

of space

earthly practicality

not always

the focus

with the four legs

of a horse

I could run

but I would

want to fly

as the released

missile could soar

but I stand posed

feet planted

bow fully

drawn

while to Chinese culture

I am the dragon

capable of fire

capable of flight

courageous intelligent

charismatic passionate

but still impetuous

sometimes inflexible

David A. Folds

they say to dragon

avoid the dog

but I married

one born

year of the dog

we have survived

and flourished

for over forty years

the archer dragon

and the libra canine

continue to find

our balance

and search together

our direction

the signs

being what they will

we bring our insides

out to meet the world

10/29/2020   Jersey City, NJ, USA

The Wind of Words

winding words through

moments of chaos

attempting to rush across

the excess of time

to meet the terminus

of thoughts

bursting forward

standing still

in all rigidity

find the focus point

expressed in certainty

the reason inescapable

this is what you mean

the artistry

of your exposition

breaths proudly

within your breast

David A. Folds

but the power

    of the presentation

floats away from

    disinterested ears

      and transient hearts

effort given

    but lost

      among the ether

10/31/2020   Jersey City, NJ, USA

Searching

I dream of a rising

of a new reality

that wanders elsewhere

lost in past or future

the moments walk or stumble

pressing onward

unrelenting

without compression

through soft mist fog

faint light

strains to break forth

but within the mire

of the unknown

all is not lost

only missing

now objects demand

discovery

David A. Folds

a need for clearing

for distinctive clarity

awaiting a change

the misty anonymous curtain

gradually thins

ghost like forms

flutter into view

not yet defined

until images sharpen

to build their strength

and a world of wonder

declares itself

the trees are left

half bare

the multi-colored

dead leaves

are strewn

without a thought

a wetness has visited

the passive pavement

now some birds

frolic in

a welcomed puddle

and the breath of life

will continue

running along

in rhythm

11/6/2020 Jersey City, NJ, USA

David A. Folds

Kanyakumari 2007

we all checked into the hotel

by midday

here at the bottom tip

of the subcontinent

dramatically facing

the confluence

of three waters

Arabian Sea to the West

Bay of Bengal to the East

and between them

stretching wider farther

the vast Indian Ocean

going out

after settling in our room

we took a ferry

full of mostly Indians

out to the island rock

memorial to the

early guru to the West

Vivekananda

here he reached

his full

enlightenment

if only that could

transfer to us

from there a ferry hop

to its neighbor rock

dominated by the towering

Valluvar statue

soaring up 133 feet

we are told he is honored

as a great Tamil poet

and philosopher

his time is unsure

but about two millennia ago

David A. Folds

back on shore

looking below us

on view were

the many varied colors

of rows

of beached wooden

fishing boats

still before dinner

we walked

above the beach

watching a few

walking along the sand

as a late afternoon moon

declared its virtue

over the rushes

of the day

at dinner

we were told that

at dawn

on our hotel roof

the birthing sun

could be on display

if we were aggressive

enough to forgo

some sleep

arising while still dark

Vickie wanted sleep

I wanted images

and drama

my camera capturing

each slight step

slowly rising up of our

flaming red-orange star

David A. Folds

once on a full morning stage

it could not impact

like its intense dawning

at this truly unique

seaside

the confluence and

the drama of the dawn

can imprint on my memory

forever

11/17/2020   Jersey City, NJ, USA

Names

though they often seem

to supersede

their object

names are later

arriving add-ons

that gain their

own reality

when I first meet

any person

a handshake or nod

completes

the connection

and the giving of names

floats in

and quickly

fades away

David A. Folds

later with repetition

a name will be

stapled to my memory

along with the

more memorable

visual image

some names seem

at odds with

their image

or in opposition to

their object's being

what to make of someone

named a number 2

or like my brother

actually a third

how does this tripling

sequence have meaning

Afloat in the Continuum

when number 1

        never knew of

        number 3

and number 2

        leans over

observing the growth

        of number 3

with little connection

I was named for

        a first settler

        of New Haven

first parent

        in a still growing

        family tree

in this once

        new European world

the New Haven Colony

        formed in 1637

seems farther from me

        than the sun

David A. Folds

but the name of

David Atwater

still resonates

inside my being

part of who I am

if not of

what I am

our names are living

attachments

that echo

in insistence

throughout our lives

like it or not

12/22/2020 Jersey City, NJ, USA

Afloat in the Continuum

A New Year

again we await the onset

of a new year

but usual thoughts of

resolutions of change

are dwarfed by unusual

needs for change

never before in my lifetime

have we looked back at

the closing of

such a year

we have seen 2020 with an

incessant flood of rising

numbers of disaster

here in the US

with 4 and a quarter percent

of the world's people

we have suffered 19 percent

of the world's covid deaths

David A. Folds

our suffering is compounded

by knowing that the extreme

failure nationally

has caused so many

of these losses

a selfish ego-centric

policy of blinders

presidency

has poisoned our chances

to contain the spread

of this scourge

a new year and

a new presidency

give rise to hope

I pray we soon can look for

a chance for a path

towards a new version

of normalcy

12/30/2020 Jersey City, NJ, USA

Index of Poems by Titles

David A. Folds

www.ingramcontent.com/pod-product-compliance
Lightning Source LLC
Chambersburg PA
CBHW031846090426
42741CB00005B/371